GW00392357

MY FIRST BOOK OF FINANCIAL EDUCATION

How to save and make your money grow

Floren Verdú

CONTENTS:

Chapter 1:

SAVINGSLAND

Once upon a time, there was a town called Savingsland. It was found in a lost place in what is now the US, and a brother and sister named Peter and Maggie lived there.

The siblings had no mother or father, and they lived with their grandfather, James. Their grandpa couldn't work because he was too old, but he was very intelligent and helped his two grandchildren out a lot.

Peter and Maggie were eight-year-old twins and they were very hardworking. Peter's job was to carry pails of water from the river to his house, which was built in the center of the town square. Maggie was a fisher girl, and every day she would catch three fish for herself and another three for her brother.

There were many people in Savingsland, and they all had to fish and to fetch water, though many of the townspeople's job was to gather fruit from the forest.

Peter and Maggie would get very tired working, and it occurred to them that there had to be a way to make their jobs easier. So, Peter decided to build a pipe that would bring water from the river to the well in the middle of the town. Since all the houses were in the town center, he thought this would be an excellent idea, since it would also make life easier for all the other townspeople.

Maggie wanted to make her job easier, too, and she decided to discuss it with her grandfather, James.

"Grandpa, I want to catch more fish with less effort, but I don't know what to do. Can you help me?" asked Maggie.

"Honey, I have heard that in some towns in the north of California they use boats and nets, but I don't know how to do that. You could travel there, and maybe someone will show you how," replied Grandpa James.

"Thank you for your help, Grandpa!"

Maggie decided to travel to the towns in northern California, because she was very adventurous and she was convinced that her grandfather was right.

She traveled for several days and finally arrived in a town called San Francisco, where she met an old man called Paul. He showed her the little boats and the nets they used for fishing. Maggie was very surprised: it was so easy to fish in San Francisco. But now, she needed to learn how to build boats and make nets.

Paul explained the manufacturing process to her. The next day, Maggie headed back to Savingsland.

A few days later, Maggie arrived home and told her brother Peter and her Grandpa James what she had learned.

Now, Peter and Maggie knew how to make their jobs easier, but they needed time, food and drink. However, the twins didn't know how to put it into practice, so they asked their Grandpa James.

"Grandpa, what can we do?" asked Maggie.

"You need to work during your free time," replied Grandpa.

"I have an idea!" said Maggie. "We could work the weekends and vacations."

"We could also sleep one hour less," said Peter.

"Both great ideas!" exclaimed Grandpa.

Maggie and Peter had to work very hard for over two years; they were soon turning ten. Peter had built a pipe that was over a thousand yards long, going went from the river to the well in the town center, and Maggie had built a little boat and a fishing net.

Peter showed the townspeople how the pipe worked, and he told them that from then on, they wouldn't have to carry pails of water any more – but in exchange, they would have to give him some of the fish they caught every month, since they no longer needed to carry pails.

Maggie, on the other hand, started fishing with her boat and net, and she could catch a lot more fish every day.

Finally, the townspeople had water every day without having to fetch it – but now, they wanted to fish like Maggie, so they talked to her about how to get boats and nets.

Maggie decided to become a builder of boats and nets, and – of course – Peter offered to help her, since he wasn't working any more.

So, Maggie started selling boats and nets, and for each boat or net she would ask for a specific number of fish – some were more expensive and some were cheaper.

Peter soon tired of eating so much fish, and he began to accept fruit from the forest in exchange for his water.

Maggie decided she could do what her brother was doing, too, so she started renting out boats and nets and asking for some of the townspeople's fish every month in return – the boats and nets would still belong to her. This meant that Maggie and Peter had a lot of passive income, and several sources of income.

Peter and Maggie had to make a lot of effort at first to build the pipe, boats and nets, but that initial effort now brings them **passive income**.

What is **passive income**?

It's money you earn without having to work – but money doesn't grow on trees, and it requires a lot of work at the beginning.

Peter and Maggie also started to earn a lot of money in different ways, since they fished, charged rent, and built boats and nets, so they had **various sources of income** rather than relying on just one wage.

Chapter 2:

BARTERING

The people of Savingsland started to have more fish, water and fruit than they needed, so people had a lot of free time.

Lots of the townspeople decided it was no longer necessary to spend their time fishing and gathering fruit from the forest and that they could do other jobs instead. This created a division of labor, where each person did a different job.

Suddenly, there were a whole bunch of different products, since people had become specialists at a lot of jobs, and in the town they now had: bread, milk, eggs, fruit, leather, and more. So, the first bakers, farmers, sellers and so on began to appear...

But, of course, now they needed somewhere to take all of those products, and so the market was created: the place where everyone took the products they had to spare.

At the market, they had to exchange one product for another, so that everyone could get what they needed – and bartering was born.

Peter went to the market to get milk, and walked up to a stall where they had a lot of it.

"Sir, I will give you ten fish for one gallon of milk," said Peter.

"Sorry, but I don't need any fish," replied the milkman.

"I understand," replied Peter. "I'll try at another stall."

The townspeople began to realize that there were sometimes problems with bartering, because some people wouldn't accept certain products simply because they didn't need them. However, there were other products that everyone wanted, which were liquid assets (wine, wheat, leather, sheep's wool, salt, and so on).

So, the problem with bartering was that some products were more in demand than others, and there was another problem, too…

Maggie went to the market to exchange salt for leather, and found a stall where they had some. When she found it, she approached the man selling leather.

"Sir, I need two leather coats. I can offer you ten pounds of salt," said Maggie.

"That doesn't seem like much salt," said the tanner. "The leather is worth more."

Maggie had encountered another problem with bartering: how did you make a fair exchange?

Bartering was a great idea, but it had some drawbacks.

DID YOU KNOW?

Liquid assets were used as the first **money**, but in order to fulfil their purpose, they needed to have certain characteristics:

- Transportable
- Divisible
- Long-lasting
- Hard to fake

Today there is a **liquid asset** that is still used as **money:** it's **gold**.

As you can see, almost anything can be used as **money**: in fact, Roman soldiers were paid in salt, which is where the word **salary** comes from.

Chapter 3:

PROPERTY, MONEY AND BILLS

Everyone in the town needed products in order to exchange them, because if you had nothing to exchange, you couldn't barter. These products that the people had were known as property, as were the houses where they lived and the land they owned, and so on.

Because when something doesn't belong to anyone, do you know what happens? No one looks after it.

In Savingsland there were a lot of trees that bore a lot of fruit, and also a lot of wild cows. But some people would chop down the trees for firewood, so there was less and less fruit. Other people hunted the cows for meat, so there came a point at which the cows were in danger of going extinct.

The mayor of Savingsland had to intervene: he told the people he was going to divide up the land around the houses into plots, and each person would be responsible for looking after whatever was on their plot of land. Because he could see that when things didn't have owners, no one looked after them. This is how property came to be.

The town was becoming famous, and merchants from all over Africa and Europe would travel there. One day, a merchant arrived in the town who was carrying little metal disks, and he headed for a stall selling wheat.

"Sir," he began. "I will give you this silver disk for a ten-pound sack of wheat."

"What is the silver disk worth?" asked the wheat seller.

"Its weight in silver, because the coin is made of silver," replied the merchant.

The wheat seller had never seen anything like it. "Where are you from?" he asked.

"From Turkey, sir."

"Okay," agreed the wheat seller. "I will accept your coin."

Soon, the town mayor found out about these little metal disks, and decided to produce his own metal disks, and so the first coins came to be.

Many other mayors heard about what had happened in Savingsland, and they decided to get together and create a common currency, and after much discussion they decided that the currency would be called the Dollar.

People began to use the coins and move around from one place to another, but they found there was a problem: the coins were heavy, and sometimes they needed to transport a lot of coins at once.

The mayors got together again, and decided to find a solution. They talked for hours and eventually came up with an idea: they would create pieces of paper stating the amount of money that the bearer would give, as well as the place where the coins would be deposited – and the first bills were born.

But now, they had another problem: where would they store all those coins? So each town created its own bank in order to store the coins, as well as gold, since the coins could also be exchanged for gold.

As you can see, money made exchanging easier in Savingsland and all over the country, and people's lives kept getting a little better.

DID YOU KNOW?

The first **coins** to be officially minted were made in Lydia (now Turkey), which was a kingdom in Asia Minor, between 680 and 560 BC.

Where were the first **bills** used?

In China in the 7th century – Marco Polo saw them when he visited the Emperor Kublai Khan in the 13th century.

What are the historical origins of the US dollar?

The story dates back to 1690, before the country was founded. The first evidence of the **Dollar** as we know it belonged to a colony in Massachusetts. The **Dollar** finally became the monetary unit of the US in 1785.

Where does the word **Dollar** come from?

It comes from the word "Thaler", which was a currency created in 1519 in Joachimsthal in Bohemia, known for its silver mines. Today, this city is part of the Czech Republican and is called Jáchymov.

In what year was the first modern **bank** created?

The first **banks** appeared in the late medieval era, around the beginning of the Renaissance, in wealthy Italian cities like Genoa and Venica. The very first bank was created in the year 1406 in Genoa, Italy. It was called the Banco di San Giorgio.

In what year was the first **bank** created in the US?

The first **bank** was created in Philadelphia (US) in 1782. It was called the **Bank of North America.**

As you can see, money doesn't just magically appear; to get it, you have to work or perform some other action.

Chapter 4:

MONEY-MAKING MACHINES

Maggie kept on making nets and boats to sell, and of course, she also continued to charge people to hire them – but she no longer got paid in fish, because people were now paying her in coins and bills. Meanwhile, Peter was receiving money for his water service.

Maggie and Peter wanted to make their businesses bigger and expand them outside of Savingsland, but they didn't know how to do it – so they went to talk to their Grandpa James.

"Grandpa, we want to take our business outside of the town, but we don't know how to do it and we also need a lot of money for it," said Maggie.

"I have an idea," he said. "Why don't you sell pieces of the company in exchange for money?"

"But Grandpa James, we don't want to lose control over our company," replied Peter. "We still want to be the bosses."

"Don't worry. You're only going to sell 49% of the company – the remaining 51% will still be yours, so you will still be the bosses."

"But how do we do that?" asked Maggie.

"Easy," replied Grandpa James. "You can make little pieces of paper in equal sizes and assign each piece of paper the same value. Then, you offer those pieces of paper to the townspeople, and the people can give you money in return for being owners of your business, too." Grandpa James went on. "But it's important that, once or twice a year, the owners of the pieces of paper get some of the earnings from your businesses."

"So, Grandpa, does that mean the people with the most pieces of paper will get the most money?" asked Peter.

"That's right, Peter – but best of all is that you two will have 51% of those pieces of paper, so you can pay yourselves, too."

"Those pieces of paper are like money-making machines!" exclaimed Peter.

"Exactly. Plus, if you do things right, those pieces of paper will get more and more valuable and you can sell them for more money – but if you do things wrong, the pieces of paper could end up worthless," warned Grandpa.

"Grandpa, wouldn't it be better for people to buy pieces of paper from a lot of businesses instead of just ours?" asked Maggie.

"Sure, Maggie. It's better not to put all of your eggs in one basket. Did you know that you can buy pieces of paper from lots of companies at once?"

"How do you do that, Grandpa?"

"Well, you buy an investment fund," explained Grandpa.

"I really like that idea," replied Maggie.

Peter and Maggie went to the market to offer people their pieces of paper, and they sold a lot of them. Then, they went to the Town Council to see if the mayor wanted some pieces of paper, too – and he did. Finally, nearly everyone in the town had some pieces of paper from Maggie and Peter's companies.

Now, the twins had enough money to expand their businesses.

Maggie started to travel, and she created even more sale and hire companies for boats and nets. Peter installed pipes in other towns, and charged them a fee for using his water service, too.

Peter, Maggie and all the people who had bought pieces of paper could now benefit from Maggie and Peter's work – the more money the twins' businesses brought in, the more the owners of the pieces of paper received. Plus, every time Peter and Maggie charged someone for a piece of paper, they reinvested that money in expanding their businesses, instead of spending it. This meant that their companies kept getting bigger.

Savingsland was growing, and it needed more and more things all the time – so the mayor decided he could have his own pieces of paper, too, in order to build and buy more things for the town.

Before long, the mayor had created his own pieces of paper – but he decided that anyone who bought them had to keep them for at least two years. The deal was that after two years, he would give them back the money they had lent him plus a little more. The townspeople really liked this idea, so lots of them bought pieces of paper from the mayor.

DID YOU KNOW?

Legend has it that there was a king from the Far East who lost his son in one of the battles waged by his army. He was so sad that nothing his subjects could offer him could make him smile.

But then, one day, someone called Sissa came to his court and asked for an audience with the king. Sissa showed him a game that he promised would make him smile and feel happy again. That game was chess.

Once he had explained the rules of the game to the king and given him a board and pieces, the king began to play, and he loved it. He played and played for hours, and a lot of his sadness disappeared. Sissa had done it.

The king was so grateful for this gift that he told Sissa to ask for anything he wanted as a reward.

> "I am rich enough to fulfil your greatest wish," said the king. "Ask for anything you want, and you shall receive it."

Sissa went quiet and thoughtful.

"Tell me your wish," insisted the king. "I will spare no expense in order to grant your request.

"Your generosity is magnificent," replied Sissa, "but please give me some time to think."

The next day, Sissa came to see the king again.

"Your Majesty, I want one grain of wheat for the first square on the chessboard, two grains for the second square, for the third four, for the fourth eight, for the fifth sixteen, for the sixth thirty-two..."

"Enough!" cried the king. "You will receive your grains of wheat in accordance with your wish. For each square on the board, double the number of grains as for the previous square, for all sixty-four squares on the chessboard. But you should know that your request is not worthy of my generosity, since you have asked for such a measly reward. You have scorned my benevolence. You should have shown more respect. Now, leave! My servants will give you the sack of wheat you have asked for."

Sissa smiled and went to wait at the door of the palace.

As he ate his evening meal, the king remembered the chess inventor and wondered if Sissa had been given that measly reward he had asked for.

"Your Majesty, we are obeying your order. The court mathematicians are calculating the number of grains we must give him," one of his servants told him.

The king frowned in annoyance.

That night, he asked once again if Sissa had left the palace yet with his sack of wheat.

> "The mathematicians are working tirelessly," his servant replied.
> "Why is this matter taking them so long?" asked the king angrily. "Tomorrow, before I wake up, I want him to have been given every last grain he asked for. I do not give orders twice."

The following morning, the chief court mathematician asked for an audience with the king so that he could deliver a very important report. Before he could speak, the king asked the old man if they had given Sissa his measly reward yet.

> "No matter the quantity, my grain stores will not be depleted," said the king.

With a quavering voice, the mathematician replied:

> "That is exactly why I have asked to see you, my lord. We have carefully calculated the number of grains Sissa requested, and I have to tell you that even with all your grain stores, and with all of those in the kingdom, and even with all of the grain stores in the world, there is not enough to fulfil the promise."

The king was astounded.

> "Tell me, old man," he said. "What is that monstruous number?".
> - Oh, my lord... 18,446,744,073,709,551,665 grains of wheat, your Majesty. All the produce from the fields over the next thousand years would not fulfil his request, my king," admitted the mathematician.

Can you imagine if we could multiply **money** as quickly as that?

I'm here to tell you that we can.

It's called **investing**.

What does **investment** mean?

It means, among other things, giving your **money** to someone for a period of time, and in exchange they give you back your **money** plus a little extra.

So, who should you lend to?

You can lend money to businesses, or even to the government in your country or another country.

How can you multiply your **money**?

I'm sure you remember that Maggie and Peter divided their businesses into equally-sized chunks, and made a little piece of paper for each chunk.

Do you know the name for those pieces of

paper?

They are called **shares**.

Do you remember that the owners of Maggie and Peter's **shares** received money?

That **money** is called **dividends**.

Do you remember that the mayor made his own pieces of paper?

Well, those pieces of paper are normally made by the governments of countries, and they are called **bonds.**

Investing involves some risks, and it's not a good idea to put all your eggs in one basket, but you can reduce this risk by buying an investment fund. Some let you buy many shares, and some let you buy from over 1,500 companies at once.

Did you know that some companies you've heard of make their own pieces of paper?

Nintendo, McDonald's, Amazon, Disney...

How much money would your grandfather have now if he had invested in **shares** many years ago?

- $1,000 in eBay in 1998 would now be worth 2,712,997 dollars.
- $1,000 in Apple in 1980 would now be worth 482,151 dollars.
- $1,000 in Microsoft in 1986 would now be worth 1,421,280 dollars.
- $1,000 in Google in 2004 would now be worth 21,672 dollars.
- $1,000 in Facebook in 2012 would now be worth 5,382 dollars.
- $1,000 in Amazon in 1997 would now be worth 1,047,914 dollars.

All these numbers would be the current value of the pieces of paper from those companies, but you need to remember that every time your grandfather had received a **dividend,** he would have 3 options:

- Spend it
- Save it
- **Reinvest it**

What does **reinvest** mean?

It means using it to buy more shares from the same company, so you can get more **dividends.**

It's the chessboard trick!
I'm sure you've realized by now that money-making machines do exist – and anyone can buy them.

But to see the real power of these money-making machines, you need to have as many as you can and – of course – leave them for many years so that they can do their work. This means **you need to start investing as**

soon as possible.

Don't worry, your mom or dad can help you – but first, they'll need to educate themselves. That's okay; they can do that just by reading a simple book.

Chapter 5:

DEFERRED GRATIFICATION

Maggie and Peter began to have a lot of money and they didn't want to waste it, but sometimes they couldn't distinguish expensive things from cheap things.

The twins decided to talk to Grandpa James about it.

"Grandpa, we have a problem. We don't want to waste our money."
"How can we tell if something's expensive, or cheap?" asked Maggie."

"That's a very good question, Maggie," replied Grandpa James. "Things are expensive or cheap depending on what value they have for us."

"What do you mean?" asked Peter. "I don't understand."

"Don't worry, Peter. I'll explain it to you. You have to learn to distinguish between price and value. Price is the money you pay for something, and value is what you get in exchange for that. Let me give you an example: A chocolate cake that costs $25 might seem cheap to me, because I love chocolate – but if I were allergic to chocolate, that cake would have no value for me, and I would find that price expensive," explained Grandpa James.

"Grandpa, is the dollar the currency of Savingsland?" queried Maggie.

"Of course, honey. You are a scatterbrain."

"Thank you for your advice, Grandpa!" said the twins.

So, Peter and Maggie decided to buy some things they really wanted and that held value for them. Maggie bought a bike, and Peter a piano – and they were both delighted with their purchases.

Peter and Maggie also wanted to buy themselves each a house, because they would soon be starting families and becoming more independent.

Peter dreamed of living on a small, uninhabited island very close to Savingsland. Maggie wanted a house with a garden and a pool.

But although they were earning a lot of money, they didn't have enough to buy the houses of their dreams – so they had to make a decision. They needed to decide whether they wanted to live in smaller houses that weren't the ones they really wanted, or to wait and get their dream homes.

Maggie and Peter decided to wait.

A few years passed, and when Maggie and Peter turned twenty, they had enough money to buy the houses they wanted. Their effort had paid off.

"Maggie, Peter, I want to talk to you!" shouted Grandpa James.

"What's the matter, Grandpa?" asked Maggie.

"You bought the houses of your dreams, and I want to congratulate you. You've done a great job, because you were able to distinguish between a need and a want. Some people don't know how to do that," said Grandpa.

"What do you mean?" said Peter

"I'll explain it to you: you and Maggie had a need, which was a home to live in. But you also had a want, which was the house of your dreams. But a need can't wait – if you're starving, you have to eat. A want, however, is different. You might want to eat chocolate chip cookies, but you're not going to starve to death if you don't get them."

"I understand now. A need is something that's essential, and a want is something you can live without," said Maggie.

"Very good, Maggie. That's right," replied Grandpa James. "You were also both able apply deferred gratification – sometimes, waiting brings you better things for the future. That said, it's not always worth waiting. If you were in the desert and you were dying of thirst, would you drink water, or would you wait? I think the answer is obvious: having a drink of water at that point would be a need, not a want. So, would you give all your money away for one bottle of water in the desert?"

"No!" exclaimed Peter. "That would be too high a price!"

"Are you sure? Imagine it had been three days since you had drunk anything, and you were about to die. What value would that bottle of water hold for you?"

"I understand now, Grandpa. Sometimes it's better to wait, and sometimes it's not. Deferred gratification allows you to get better things for the future, but sometimes you can't wait," said Maggie.

"I think you get it now," replied Grandpa James.

DID YOU KNOW?

Imagine that you were left alone in a room with some candyfloss or other treat you really liked, and told that in fifteen minutes, someone would come back and give you two of that treat if you could wait that long without eating it.

What would you do? Would you eat it, or wait and get two?

This was a study that measured **deferred gratification** in children; in this situation, it is better to wait.

This test was done in the late sixties and early seventies, devised by a psychologist called Walter Mischel. It is known as "the marshmallow experiment".

Chapter 6:

NEVER SPEND MORE THAN YOU MAKE!

Everyone in Savingsland knew that Maggie and Peter had money, and sometimes people would go and ask them for some of it. The twins quickly realized that they could lend people money, and then charge them interest on it.

Morgan, one of their neighbors, went to Peter's house to ask him for some money.

"Mister Peter," said Morgan. "I have a problem. I owe a lot of money, because I spend everything I make and I never save anything."

"And what can I do for you?" asked Peter.

"I need you to lend me a thousand dollars, please."

"Okay," said Peter. "But you will have to give me some interest. I'll lend you $1000, but a month from now, you will have to give me back $1,100."

"I understand. No problem," replied Morgan.

The following month, Morgan found he couldn't pay off his debt – and he went to Peter to ask for more money.

"Peter, I don't have the money. I need some more."

"How much do you need?" Peter asked.

"I need two thousand dollars. That way, I can pay you the 1,100 that I owe you, and have nine hundred left over."

"Okay, Morgan. But you need to remember that you will also have to pay interest on the two thousand dollars. That means that the next time you come, you will have to give me $2,200," said Peter.

Morgan worked as the town carpenter, and he was doing well – in fact, he was earning more and more money all the time. But the more money he made, the more he spent – and he never saved anything because he was always buying cool things he found for sale. Morgan always had the latest computers, phones, cars, videogames, and more. He didn't care what they cost, because he could always borrow more money.

Morgan didn't just owe Peter money – he also owed money to the bank, because he had loans and credit cards, and he owed money to other townspeople, too.

Morgan had to sell all his property in order to pay off all his debts, and there came a point at which he had nothing left to sell.

Finally, poor Morgan went bankrupt and was ruined – he hadn't known that he should never spend more than he had, and he hadn't known that it wasn't a good idea to borrow money.

DID YOU KNOW?

One warm fall day, Oliver and Ashley were arguing:

"Those are my chestnuts!" cried Ashley.

"I helped you get them, so I should be able to eat half of them," said Oliver.

"Neither of you should eat all of the chestnuts," said their grandpa.

"Neither of us?!" exclaimed Ashley.

"Why not?" asked Oliver.

"Let me tell you a story about bears and monkeys," said their grandpa. "One summer, many years ago, the monkeys had their best ever crop of bananas. They were so happy eating as many bananas as they wanted. They even wasted the bananas by throwing them at each other. But, one day, it stopped raining – and the bananas ran out. The monkeys were beginning to get hungry. Fortunately for them, their bear friends acted like heroes: instead of eating all the forest fruits, the bears were very smart and they stored the fruit for later. They only ate what they needed to survive. When the bears awoke from their hibernation and saw the terrible situation that the monkeys were in, they decided to help them out. From that year on, the monkeys realized that they couldn't waste their bananas playing with them or feasting on them, so they started to put away two out of every ten bananas they gathered. This way, they still had more than enough bananas to eat," explained the grandfather.

"Those monkeys weren't too smart," said Oliver.

"I don't want to end up like those monkeys, with nothing to eat," added Ashley.

Their grandfather smiled. "So, for every ten chestnuts you find, put away two – that way, when there are fewer to go around, you'll have some extra chestnuts. And I haven't told you the best part yet: when you put your chestnuts away, they don't just stay there. They grow into trees. And those trees give more and more chestnuts, and the more you wait, the more you'll get."

"I can't wait to start saving our chestnuts," said Oliver.

"Maybe one day, we'll have enough chestnuts to help our friends out like the bears did," Ashley added.

Both children and adults need to do what the animals of the forest do, and learn to **save two out of every ten coins we get,** because we never know when we're going to need them.

So, we have learned that:

- **Spending all the money we have is easy, but dangerous.**
- **Borrowing money is nearly always a bad idea – you end up owing more and more each time.**
- **Every decision we make in life has consequences.**

Chapter 7:

ALLOWANCES

Maggie and Peter were very happy in Savingsland, and they had a lot of friends there. For years, Peter had been in love with his friend Madison, and one day he decided to tell her how he felt.

Peter and Madison quickly realized that they had a lot in common, and that they were happier together than they were apart. So they decided to get married and live together in Peter's house on the island.

After a few happy years together, they decided to have a child, and Adam was born. He was a very naughty and impulsive child.

Maggie was a good girl who was popular among her friends. She also really liked a guy called Jack, so she asked him to come live with her in her house with the garden and pool. He accepted without hesitating, since he really liked Maggie, too.

Maggie and Jack didn't get married, but they decided to have a child: a daughter named Chloe, who was very quiet and responsible.

Luckily, there were schools in Savingsland, so Chloe and Adam went to classes and learned lots of things.

But Peter and Maggie realized that school wasn't teaching their kids anything about money.

They were so worried that they decided to go and talk to their Grandpa James.

"Grandpa," began Maggie. "We have a problem. We don't want Chloe and Adam to grow up to be like Morgan."

"Is Morgan the man from the town who went bankrupt?" asked Grandpa James.

"That's right!" exclaimed Peter.

"Grandpa, we have realized that school isn't giving our kids any financial education."

"Of course it's not!" replied Grandpa. "Their mothers and fathers should be teaching them those things at home."

"Grandpa James, what can we do?" asked Peter.

"Well," said Grandpa. "I would give them a weekly allowance."

"You would give Chloe and Adam a weekly allowance?" clarified Maggie.

"That's right, that's what I said."

"What if they spend all their money on candy?" asked Peter.

"It doesn't matter. You have to let them make their own mistakes. It's better for them to make mistakes now, with small amounts of money, than with the mortgage on their houses later," replied Grandpa James.

"Okay," said Maggie. "We understand."

"Thank you Grandpa!"

When Chloe and Adam reached eight years of age, they received their first real allowances – up until then, all they had ever received were a few loose coins here and there. Chloe was getting ten one-dollar coins, and Adam the same.

Chloe, who was very responsible, decided to save all her money. Adam was mischievous, and spent it all on candy.

Peter and Maggie called the children together to talk to them.

"Chloe and Adam, you've both done things wrong," began Maggie.

"But I saved all of my allowance!" cried Chloe.

"Yes, Chloe," replied her mother. "But you can't save your entire allowance, or you'll become mean and stingy."

"And what did I do wrong?" asked Adam.

"The only thing you've done right is spend your money on something you really like – the problem is, you spent it all," explained Peter.

"So, what are we supposed to do?" asked Chloe.

"From now on," he said, "you will have three piggybanks. One will be for savings or investment, one for donating, and one for spending. In the savings and investment piggybank, you will put at least two out of every ten coins. In the donation one, at least one out of ten. And in the spending one, put whatever you have left. And this is important: you must put some coins in the spending piggybank. You must follow this order: savings and investment, donations, and spending."

"Do you understand?" asked Maggie.

"Yes," said Chloe. "We have to save two out of every ten coins, like in the story of the squirrels and the chestnuts."

"And donate one coin to people in need," added Adam, "and spend the rest on candy, toys or whatever we want.

"But we have to follow the order you have taught us," said Chloe.

"That's right, Chloe and Adam!" exclaimed Peter and Maggie.

Chloe took note of Peter and Maggie's instructions, and there came a point at which she had enough money to buy herself some skates that cost a hundred dollars. However, she decided to wait a year to be sure she was going to use them enough. After a year, she went to the store to buy them.

But there was an unpleasant surprise in store for Chloe: the price of the skates had gone up to two hundred dollars.

But it had only been a year!

What had happened?

Well, the "inflation monster" had eaten Chloe's money.

DID YOU KNOW?

Your **allowance** is just like your parents' salaries, and you need to learn to use it properly.

So that you don't spend all your **money**, but also so that you don't save it all, you need to have **three piggybanks**:

1. **Savings/investment**
2. **Donation**
3. **Spending**

You can use the **money** in the **savings piggybank** for:

- **Saving it** in the bank or piggybank.
- **Investing it** to make it grow.
  Remember the **money-making** machines?

Why do you need to **save money**?
So that you never end up like the monkeys in the story. Because when you're older, at

some point you may end up with no job or you might have an emergency.

Why should you **invest**?

To make your **money** grow, and so that the **inflation monster** doesn't eat it.

Remember what happened to Chloe with the skates?

I'm going to explain what the **inflation monster** is. It means that every year, the same things get more expensive.

So, with the same amount of **money,** you will be able to buy less and less stuff.

What can you **invest** in?

- Your own business.
- Your education.
- Real estate (houses, stores, etc.
- Physical objects that go up in value: like gold.

- Shares in companies and government bonds.
- Investment funds.

The **money** in the **donation piggybank** can be used for:

- Helping homeless people you see in the street.
- Donating to charity: Save the Children, Greenpeace, Partners in Health, and so on.

You can use the **money** in the **spending piggybank** for:

- Buying toys or candy, giving your mom or dad a gift, helping to pay for your birthday party, and more.

Let me give you a **tip** for never ending up with no money: **always save first!**

Because when you're older, if you wait to save what you have left over, **you will never have anything left over!**

CHAPTER 8:

WISHLISTS AND BUDGETING

Chloe and Adam had learned how to use their three piggybanks, and now they had enough money saved up in their savings, but they didn't want to rush into buying things. They were so concerned that they went to speak to Peter and Maggie about it.

"Dad, Aunt Maggie, we don't know what to do with our spending money, because we don't want to regret the things we buy," said Adam.

"Adam, I'm so glad you've changed and become so responsible!" exclaimed Peter.

"Your dad is right," said his Aunt Maggie. "What about you, Chloe – do you know what you want to spend the money in your spending piggybank on?"

"No, Mom," she replied. "I have the same problem as Adam."

"Don't worry – we're going to give you some tips," said Peter.

"From now on, you're going to make a wishlist," said Maggie.

"What is that?" asked Adam.

"A wishlist is a piece of paper where you write down all the things you want to have, and it's very important that you don't buy anything that hasn't been on the wishlist for at least a week."

"And what is the point of the wishlist?" asked Chloe.

"Well," explained Maggie, "it will stop you from impulse buying, which is when you buy things you're not going to use."

"Like Maggie says, these are things you don't really need but that you buy because you saw someone else with them or you saw them in commercials," said Peter.

"But worst of all," added Maggie, "is that you buy these things thinking that they are going to make you happy, but all they do is waste your money. Because most of these things will be worth less after you buy them."

"So we can't buy things we're excited about getting?" asked Adam.

"Of course you can, but whatever you buy needs to have been on your wishlist for at least a week."

"Also," Peter continued, "your mom or dad may decide to buy you something that's on your wishlist, so it's good for that, too. You will learn a very important lesson by using the wishlist: sometimes, it's worth waiting and getting something better in the future."

"I'm sure I could have avoided buying a lot of useless things if I had had a wishlist!" exclaimed Maggie.

When Chloe and Adam went to the grocery store, they sometimes bought things that weren't on their wishlists, but they were low-cost items. Every time they were going to make a more expensive purchase, they would first add it to their wishlist and, of course, they never bought anything that hadn't been on the list for at least one week. Sometimes, they had to save up in order to buy things, but they didn't mind because they were worth waiting for. However, they came to realize that in order to buy more expensive things, they had to plan for them so they went to speak to Peter and Maggie once again.

"Mom, Uncle Peter, we want to have a joint birthday party," said Chloe.

"But we don't know how to do it or how much money we will need. We don't even know how much money we can spend on it," added Adam.

"Of course you don't know yet," said Maggie. "You need a budget."

"A what?" asked Adam.

"A budget," said Peter.

"And what is that?" asked Chloe.

"Do we need to study?" said Adam.

"No, don't worry," replied Maggie.

"You need to know how to add and subtract," explained Peter. "And you also need to know how much income you have and how much money you will spend."

"But what income do we have?" asked Chloe.

"Your allowance."

"But our allowances are small," protested Adam. "We're not going to be able to get enough money to have our birthday party."

"You will have to save up. Between you and Chloe, you can do it," said Maggie.

"Your parents can give you a donation, too – include that in your budget," added Peter. "Remember that you have to note down all your income and expenses."

"You should also know that you can use the budget to calculate how long it will take you to reach your goal," said Maggie.

"Yes," continued Peter. "Until you create some budgets, you won't know how to do it by yourselves and you will have to ask for help from your parents."

"I understand," said Chloe. "We need to make a plan in order to buy things."

"That's right, but it's not just to buy things – the plan will also be important when you're older and you have your own houses," said Maggie.

"Thank you for your help!" chorused Adam and Chloe.

"You're welcome," replied Maggie and Peter.

Chloe and Adam saved up for ten months and had their joint birthday party, but they couldn't invite all the children in their class because they didn't have enough money. However, the most important thing was that they reached their goal.

From then on, Adam and Chloe would create a budget every time they wanted to buy something expensive from their wishlists, but they loved doing it, because it meant they always knew how long it would take them to get the toys they wanted.

DID YOU KNOW?

We have learned about making **wishlists** so that we don't rush into buying things, and that to buy something expensive, it needs to be on the **wishlist** for at least a week first. We also learned that we pay for all the things we want from our **spending** piggybank.

Now, I want to teach you two rules you should apply when buying things:

1. **Learn deferred gratification (being able to wait, when it's worth doing so).**
2. **Never spend more than you make.**

I also need you to understand two very important things:

1. **If you spend more than you have or make, you will get into debt.**
2. **If your income is more than your spending, you will have savings.**

Unfortunately, you have to choose one of these two paths – but I really hope you will choose the second path so that you don't end up like Morgan, who went bankrupt because he spent more than he had.

Finally, we also learned how to use **budgets,** and we know that with good **planning,** we can achieve anything we want.

Chapter 9:

JOBS OF THE FUTURE

Adam and Chloe turned eighteen and started to think about their future jobs. Luckily for them, they hadn't had to work as children, whereas Peter and Maggie had begun working at just eight years old.

Years had passed and things had changed a lot, and eventually, the internet arrived in Savingsland. It was a very important step, because it was going to change the world and the world of work.

The internet brought jobs to Savingsland that hadn't existed before, as well as changing some jobs that did already exist.

Adam and Chloe didn't want to make a mistake when choosing their careers, so they went to speak to Peter and Maggie.

"We want to find a job that has a future and makes a lot of money," Adam told them.

"Why do you need to find a job? Has it occurred to you that maybe you could make one?"

"What do you mean, make a job?" asked Chloe.

"Well, Chloe, it's great to look for work, because you might find a job you really like – but it's not the only way. You can also create your own job, and be your own boss," explained Maggie.

"And why do you need to make a lot of money from your job?" wondered

Peter. "If you earn a lot, that's great. But it's not the most important thing. The most important thing is that you do a job you like."

"You know what the best thing would be?" said Maggie.

"What's that?" asked Chloe.

"For you to turn your hobbies into your future careers. That way, you'll make money for something you enjoy."

"What a cool idea!" exclaimed Adam and Chloe.

"So, how do we learn about the things we're interested in?" asked Adam.

"You have a lot of options, but I would look online: books, news articles, videos…And I would also learn about marketing and sales, because all jobs will require you to sell something. It might not be a job – sometimes, what you're selling is yourself."

"Sell ourselves?!" cried Chloe. "What do you mean?"

"We all have a personal brand online. We share photos and information, we write things. All of these things that we do online create our personal brand, and we have to take care over that, because sometimes it can cause problems. So, you can have a great personal brand that makes people want to hire you or work for you, or you can have a bad personal brand, where no one wants to work with you and no one will hire you," explained Maggie.

"I think I understand now. If I want to get a job, I have to convince the person interviewing me to hire me. So I would be the product. And if I've written bad things online or posted bad photos, my personal brand will be bad and it could hurt me in the future. If I want to do door-to-door selling, I will have to convince people to buy my product, and in that case then the thing I am selling would be an actual product. So, for all these reasons, we have to learn how to sell," said Chloe.

"Very good, Chloe. I think you've understood it," replied Maggie.

"Adam, have you?" asked Peter.

"Yes, Aunt Maggie and Chloe explained it very well," said Adam. "But why do we have to learn about marketing?"

"Because nowadays, almost all advertising is done online, and if you don't buy advertising, no one will know who you are. Imagine you had the best candy shop in the world in your house," said Maggie, "but no one knew it was there. Would you sell any candy?"

"No," replied Adam. "No one would know about it."

"Well, that's what marketing is for," explained Peter.

"Thank you, Dad and Aunt Maggie!"

"Thanks! I learned a lot, too," added Chloe.

"You're welcome," replied Peter and Maggie.

Adam and Chloe carried on studying at high school, and – of course – enjoying their free time. Adam loved playing videogames, while Chloe loved planes, birds and anything that flew.

After a year thinking about the words of Peter and Maggie, Adam decided to become a videogame designer, and Chloe started flying a drone.

A few years later, Adam had designed his first videogame and Chloe had become a drone pilot.

Adam funded his first videogame design company and started earning a lot of money – he also sometimes worked for other companies, but what he liked best was being his own boss.

Chloe, for her part, founded a transport company using drones rather than trucks. She became her own boss, too, and had a lot of fun. And when she had enough time, she also took part in professional league drone racing

Grandpa James, Maggie, Peter, Jack, Madison, Chloe and Adam were very happy, and they never had any financial problems.

It's time for us to say goodbye – but don't be sad, because we'll see each other soon. Hugs to you.

DID YOU KNOW?

Thanks to the internet, new **jobs** have appeared that didn't exist before, such as:

- Designing videogames.
- Designing cellphone apps.
- Flying drones.
- Managing businesses' social media.
- Selling products or services online without having a physical store or face-to-face customer service.
- Repairing 3D printers.
- Manufacturing and repairing robots.

Did you know that some companies have fired employees because of comments they made on social media?

Did you know that some companies check your social media pages before hiring you?

Did you know you could lose out on an important sale because of comments you make on social media?

You must take care over your **personal brand** and be very careful about what you write and post to social media, because it can't be deleted.

It's also very important that you learn about **sales and marketing,** since you'll need these for any job.

It would also be fantastic to turn your hobby into your **job,** so that going to work doesn't feel like a chore for you.

I want to tell you that, while you need to pass high school, don't worry if you don't want to go to college – it's not the only path. Remember, we also need: plumbers, electricians, gardeners, business owners...

Finally, don't forget that **you don't have to work for a company, because you can create your own business and be your own boss.**

RECOMMENDATIONS

If you really liked this book, I also recommend that you read three great books – I didn't write them, but you'll love them:

1. *My first book of economics, saving and investments.* By María Jesús Soto.

2. *How to Turn $100 into $1.000.000: Earn! Save! Invest!* By James McKenna.

3. *Finance 101 for Kids: Money lessons children cannot afford to miss.* By Walter Andal.

Finally, I would be very grateful if you would leave me a positive review on Amazon. Thank you very much.

Printed in Great Britain
by Amazon

75728662R00061